EXTREME MACHINES

THE WORLD'S MOST UNUSUAL MACHINES

Paloma Jae

Raintree

www.raintreepublishers.co.uk
Visit our website to find out more information about Raintree books.

To order:
☎ Phone 0845 6044371
🖨 Fax +44 (0) 1865 312263
💻 Email myorders@raintreepublishers.co.uk

Customers from outside the UK please telephone +44 1865 312262

Raintree is an imprint of Capstone Global Library Limited, a company incorporated in England and Wales having its registered office at 7 Pilgrim Street, London, EC4V 6LB – Registered company number: 6695582

Edited by Nancy Dickmann and Megan Cotugno
Designed by Jo Hinton-Malivoire
Picture research by Tracy Cummins
Originated by Capstone Global Library
Printed and bound in China by CTPS

ISBN 978 1 406216 91 2 (hardback)
15 14 13 12 11
10 9 8 7 6 5 4 3 2 1

British Library Cataloguing in Publication Data
Jae, Paloma.
The world's most unusual machines. -- (Extreme machines)
629'.046-dc22
A full catalogue record for this book is available from the British Library.

Acknowledgments
We would like to thank the following for permission to reproduce photographs: Alamy p. **23** (© Phil Taplin); AP Photo pp. **6** (Gareth Fuller/PA Wire), **7** (Gareth Fuller/PA Wire), **18** (HEINZ DUCKLAU), **24** (Shuji Kajiyama), **26** (Anja Niedringhaus); Corbis pp. **4** (© Roland Weihrauch/dpa), **10** (© Transtock), **11** (© Bettmann), **13** (© Reuters), **22** (© Rainer Schimm/Messe Essen/epa); Getty Images pp. **15** (STR/AFP), **16** (ChinaFotoPress/), **25** (YOSHIKAZU TSUNO/AFP), **27** (FABRICE COFFRNI/AFP); Honda pp. **8, 9**; Rinspeed Inc. pp. **17, 19** (Dingo/H. Streit/Jeebee); U.S. Navy p. **14** (Chief Petty Officer Alan Baribeau); p. **12** wheelsurf (www.wheelsurf.nl); Zuma Press pp. **5** (© Jose M. Osorio/Sacramento Bee), **20** (© Bandphoto/UPPA), **21** (© Bartlomiej Zborowski).

Cover photograph of the World Hovercraft Championships reproduced with permission of Getty Images (Stu Forster).

Every effort has been made to contact copyright holders of any material reproduced in this book. Any omissions will be rectified in subsequent printings if notice is given to the publisher.

Disclaimer
All the Internet addresses (URLs) given in this book were valid at the time of going to press. However, due to the dynamic nature of the Internet, some addresses may have changed, or sites may have changed or ceased to exist since publication. While the author and Publishers regret any inconvenience this may cause readers, no responsibility for any such changes can be accepted by either the author or the Publishers.

Some words are shown in bold, like this. You can find out what they mean by looking in the glossary.

Contents

How unusual!

Have you ever seen something drive past that you couldn't believe? Maybe it was a car shaped like a sausage. Maybe it was a truck that went underwater. Some of these weird machines do a special job. Others were just made for fun!

Why do you think these machines were built?

Pedalling across the sky

Want to fly and get some exercise at the same time? Try a **blimp** powered by pedalling. Hot air inside the blimp makes it float. The pedals turn a **propeller** that can make it go up to 20 kph (12 mph).

EXTREME FACT

The driver of this blimp tried to pedal across the English Channel. But the wind blew him back!

Tomorrow's unicycle

This small machine is a **unicycle** with a motor. The Honda U3X can move in any direction. You just lean your body. This is a good machine for moving inside. Just don't try to go down the stairs!

9

The monowheel

Ever wondered what driving is like from a wheel's point of view? You can find out by riding a **monowheel**, which means "one wheel." Drivers sit inside the wheel. It can move at more than 80 kph (50 mph)!

EXTREME FACT
People thought of ideas for monowheels back in the 1800s.

There are many different types of monowheel. The one below is powered by a motor. Others are pedalled like bikes. You turn them by leaning in different directions.

This monowheel is called the "Wheelsurf," because riding it feels like surfing on land!

By land or by sea

Some machines can go almost anywhere. **Amphibious** trucks can go on land or on water. Some are used by the military. They can take people and equipment from a ship to the land. Or they can attack a beach from the water. Then they drive on to the beach.

EXTREME FACT
Amphibious machines can drive straight on to a ship!

The Adventure Duck gives tours of China by land and sea.

Amphibious cars and trucks can be used for many things. Some give tours on land and water. Others are just driven for fun. Some cars and trucks can be **adapted** to use in water. But they need to be waterproof, and they need to float!

This machine is called the Surface **Orbiter**. A man called Rick Dobbertin built it to drive over land and sea. He spent more than two years going halfway around the world!

↑ The Surface Orbiter was built from a tank used to carry milk!

EXTREME FACT

You need **scuba gear** to drive this car.
It can go as deep as 9 metres under
the water! It was built without a roof so
people could get out in an emergency.

Blowing by

A **hovercraft** drives on land or water. But it has no wheels, and it hardly even touches the ground! It uses fans to move around. A fan at the bottom blows into the ground. This keeps it "floating." Another fan at the back pushes it forward.

These drivers are racing in the Hovercraft Championship.

Art on wheels

Some unusual cars are made just to turn heads. They might be made to look like an object, such as a shoe or a dinosaur. Or they might be covered with something strange, such as grass.

⬆ This scary car was created by the artist William Burge. He called it "Phantoms."

This car is shaped like a dolphin!

Low rider

Big cars use a lot of energy. But not this car! The Oxyride Racer is so small, you could walk over it. It is so low that the wind doesn't slow it down. It doesn't need much energy. It runs on batteries you could buy in a shop!

There isn't much room in the Oxyride Racer!

Rocket man

Yves Rossy wanted to fly without using an aeroplane. So he built a wing with a jet pack on it. He strapped it to his back and took off. Yves flew 35 kilometres across the English Channel. It took him less than 10 minutes!

EXTREME FACT

With wings on his back, Yves Rossy can fly at speeds of up to 300 kph (186 mph)!

Test yourself!

Try to match each question to the correct answer.

① Honda U3X

② Hovercraft

③ Amphibious machines

④ Oxyride Racer

⑤ Surface Orbiter

a Which machine is powered by batteries?

b Which machine is powered by fans?

c What military vehicles can go on land or water?

d Which machine moves when you lean forward?

e What was built from a tank used to carry milk?

Glossary

adapted changed to use in another way

amphibious able to drive on land or in water

blimp vehicle that floats through the air

hovercraft machine that is powered by fans

monowheel machine with one wheel a that driver sits inside

orbiter a machine that goes around something, such as the Earth

propeller spinning blade that pushes through air or water

scuba gear equipment that allows breathing underwater

unicycle cycle with only one wheel

Find out more

Books

Go!, Samone Bos, Phil Hunt, Andrea Mills (Dorling Kindersley, 2006)

Hovercraft, Aaron Sautter (Capstone Press, 2007)

Concept Cars, Jeffrey Zuehlke (Lerner Publishing, 2007)

Websites

Nissan Pivo 2
http://www.nissan-global.com/EN/PIVO2/
Learn all about the Nissan Pivo 2.

More on hovercraft
http://www.hovercraft-museum.org
Visit the hovercraft museum website to find out about different types of hovercraft and watch a video of the Hovershow.

Amphibious machines and hovercrafts
http://library.thinkquest.org/04oct/00450/index1.htm
Learn more about these machines on this website built by school children.

Find out

How fast can a hovercraft go?

Index